Coping™

COPING WITH

HATE CRIMES

Jill Robi

New York

Published in 2019 by The Rosen Publishing Group, Inc.
29 East 21st Street, New York, NY 10010

Library of Congress Cataloging-in-Publication Data

Names: Robi, Jill, author.
Title: Coping with hate crimes / Jill Robi.
Description: New York : Rosen Publishing, 2019 | Series: Coping | Audience: Grades 7–12. | Includes bibliographical references and index.
Identifiers: LCCN 2018017291| ISBN 9781508183228 (library bound) | ISBN 9781508183211 (pbk.)
Subjects: LCSH: Hate crimes—Juvenile literature.
Classification: LCC HV6773.5 .R63 2019 | DDC 364.15—dc23
LC record available at https://lccn.loc.gov/2018017291

Manufactured in China

CONTENTS

INTRODUCTION...4

CHAPTER ONE
Identifying a Hate Crime.................................8

CHAPTER TWO
Causes and Effects of Hate Crimes.......................25

CHAPTER THREE
Hate Groups in the United States.....................39

CHAPTER FOUR
Responding to Hate Crimes...........................56

CHAPTER FIVE
Changing the Culture of Hate.......................74

GLOSSARY   96
FOR MORE INFORMATION   99
FOR FURTHER READING   102
BIBLIOGRAPHY   104
INDEX   108

In the early hours of the morning of December 10, 2017, Jason and Victoria Chapa were on their way home from a family gathering. They decided to make a quick stop to look at a property in a developing area of their hometown of Marion, Texas, which they were considering purchasing. As they walked around the house, they heard the sound of glass shattering and ran back to their vehicle. What they found was shocking.

A woman named Melissa Shelton was using a shard of concrete to smash in the back windshield of their car while screaming racial slurs at the couple and saying they were too poor to move into her neighborhood. Jason Chapa is Mexican American, Victoria Chapa is African American, and Melissa Shelton is white.

When the Chapas called 911, police officers arrived at the scene but they did not issue Shelton a citation or take any action. "The neighborhood housing

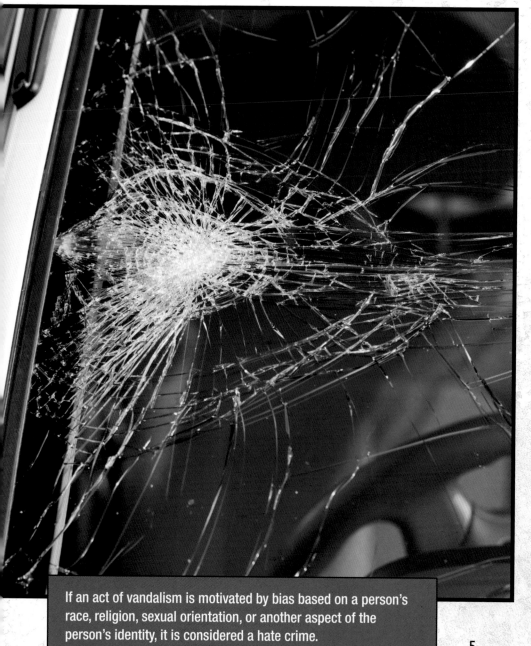

If an act of vandalism is motivated by bias based on a person's race, religion, sexual orientation, or another aspect of the person's identity, it is considered a hate crime.

association, the local realtors, all offered nothing but a silent endorsement of the attack," said attorney S. Lee Merritt, who represented the Chapas. "This was not Black History Month. This is not black history. This didn't happen 50 years ago. It happened a few weeks ago. This is America 2018." After public outcry, the Marion Police Department handed over the police report to the District Attorney's office, and Shelton was eventually indicted.

According to the Federal Bureau of Investigation's (FBI) annual Hate Crimes Statistics report, there were 6,121 hate crimes reported in 2016. This is an average of more than sixteen hate crimes a day, and it represents a 5 percent increase from 2015 and a 10 percent increase from 2014. A hate crime is a term used for a crime that is committed against someone due to an aspect of the victim's identity, such as race or ethnicity, religious beliefs, sexual orientation, disability, or gender identity. Hate crimes can include acts of violence or assault, name calling (both in person or online), and vandalism to property.

A hate crime goes beyond the act of violence itself; it affects an entire community. A hate crime is not an isolated incident, but part of a system in which marginalized groups of people fear for their safety merely because of who they are. People who have been the victims of hate crimes, or whose communities are regularly impacted by hate crimes, often suffer from PTSD or experience ongoing fear and trauma.

Addressing hate crimes begins with understanding the root of the problem and working to change the culture of hate, bigotry, and prejudice that thrives in communities across the United States. By examining the history of hate crimes in America, it is possible to gain a better understanding of the current situation.

There are a number of resources across the country that provide support for victims of hate crimes and their communities. There are also organizations and advocates working to change the culture of hate. Often this type of work begins with people organizing locally to raise awareness of prejudice in their own schools, workplaces, and communities. By learning about the history, scale, and impacts of hate crimes in the United States, you can learn to be part of the solution and work toward changing the culture of hate.

CHAPTER ONE

Identifying a Hate Crime

The Merriam-Webster dictionary defines hate crimes as "any of various crimes (such as assault or defacement of property) when motivated by hostility to the victim as a member of a group (such as one based on color, creed, gender, or sexual orientation)." Hate crimes cover a broad spectrum of incidents, including physical assault, homicide, mass shootings, sexual assault, rape, vandalism, symbolic acts, verbal abuse, and online harassment.

Hate crimes are caused by prejudice against specific groups of people based on inherent aspects of their identities, such as race, religion, sexual orientation, gender, gender identity, and disability. The FBI notes that "Hate itself is not a crime—and the FBI is mindful of protecting freedom of speech and other civil liberties." However, when a person commits a crime that is motivated by hate, that is a hate crime.

A noose is a visual symbol connected to lynching in the United States. This symbol of hate is used to threaten and intimidate African Americans.

Types of Hate Crimes

A hate crime can occur anywhere—in the workplace, at school, in a park, on public transit, on social media, in an email, in printed materials, or elsewhere. A good number of hate crimes go unreported to police, especially if they are nonviolent. Often, the victim may not even be aware that a hate crime has occurred.

Verbal Abuse and Online Harassment

Verbal abuse and online harassment count as crimes when they include a threat that the victim has a reasonable fear will be carried out. Harassment can occur in many forms, including phone calls, texting, or even posts on Facebook. Even if intended as a joke, making a threatening statement regarding a person's race, gender, religion, sexual orientation, or disability can be considered a hate crime. Abusive language is often identified as being motivated by hate if the threat includes a slur—an insulting name used to denigrate people based on their

When communities come together to protest discrimination, it sends a strong message that hate will not be tolerated.

identity—or if the perpetrator uses statements that make negative generalizations based on groups of people, for example, "you people."

Online messages, tweets, social media posts, emails, pictures, videos, website pages, and even music lyrics can be used to insult specific groups of people. Social media provides a new platform for the spreading of hate speech on the internet. Online attacks are a growing problem and can at times be hard to pinpoint. Perpetrators can hide behind fake names, profiles, and avatars. Still, these incidents should be taken seriously by police, particularly if there is a threat of violence or they include an incitement for others to use violence against a person or group of people.

Seyi Akiwowo, a Labour Party representative in the United Kingdom, received online racist and gender-based slurs in February 2017. She told BBC Radio London, "They're not just words. They actually echo the behavior we don't tolerate in society, so we shouldn't start thinking it's okay to say on any platform, on social media and the internet." In England and Wales, online hate crimes are now treated as seriously as offline offenses by the Crown Prosecution Service.

Vandalism and Symbolic Acts

Vandalism is the defacement or destruction of private or public property. If such vandalism targets a group of people or an individual based on the person's identity, it counts as a hate crime. Such examples include writing or spray painting slurs on a property, or any type of vandalism or property damage that is motivated by bias.

Vandalism can also include symbolic acts that may not cause physical damage but are used to intimidate or threaten an individual or group of people. Some examples include instances of hateful taunting with historic symbolism, such as nooses hung from trees, burning crosses, and leaving a banana for a black person. Although such acts do not involve physical contact or harm, they are still violent, because they are used to threaten and instill fear in the victim or victims, and the broader community that is the target of the hate.

Sexual Assault and Rape

Some people argue that sexual assault and rape are always hate crimes, because sexual violence is a tool used to sustain the subordination of women. Women and LGBTQ people are disproportionately victims of sexual assault and rape, and this assault is often accompanied by misogynist, homophobic, or transphobic slurs. Katherine Chen, a feminist legal scholar, argues that "men who commit gender-bias crimes seek to maintain power and dominance over women through sexual terrorism, reinforcing socially constructed views about the nature of men and women, vent their personal frustrations, exert superior status in comparison to other men, or punish women who choose to compete in areas traditionally reserved for men" according to a 2017 blog post on the National Organization for Women's website. Including gender bias in hate crimes legislation helps to extend sentencing for perpetrators of sexual violence and also sheds light on sexual violence as part of a systemic problem based in misogyny, which is the hatred of women.

Homicide

When a homicide is determined to have been motivated by bias, it is considered a hate crime. As a result, punishments for the perpetrators of these homicides are harsher than they would be in a simple homicide case. Hate crime homicides can include attacks on individuals, such as the murder of James Byrd Jr., which was motivated by racism, and the murder of Matthew Shepherd, which was motivated by homophobia. It can also include incidents of mass murder, such as the 2015 Charleston church shooting, in which white supremacist Dylann Roof walked into a church in Charleston, South Carolina, and killed nine people with an assault rifle. He later admitted he had targeted that church because he

Hate Crimes by the Numbers

According to statistics compiled by the FBI:

- There were 6,063 hate crimes in 2016, with 57.5 percent of those incidents motivated by the victim's race. This represented an increase from 2015, when there were 5,818 incidents reported, 56.9 percent of which were motivated by race.

- There were 7,509 victims of single-bias hate crime incidents in 2016.

- Nearly 59 percent of the victims (of these single-bias crimes) were targeted for their race, 21.1 percent were targeted for their religion, and 16.7 percent were targeted due to their sexual orientation.

- The number of hate crimes reported in 2016 rose 4.6 percent from 2015.

- Of the 1,538 religious bias hate crimes reported in 2016, 54.2 percent were anti-Jewish and 24.8 percent were anti-Islamic/Muslim.

wanted to kill black people and hoped to incite a race war.

History of Hate Crimes Legislation

The term "hate crime" was first used by journalists in the 1980s in an attempt to describe multiple violent incidents targeting African Americans, Asians, and Jews, but the term has been retroactively applied to crimes committed before that date, including the genocide of Jews by the Nazis in Europe in the 1940s and the persecution of Christians in Ancient Rome. The FBI investigated what are now known as hate crimes as far back as World War One, and its role was amplified after the Civil Rights Act was passed in 1964. Prior to that, the FBI held the position that protecting civil rights was not a federal function but a local one.

The first federal hate crimes statute was signed into law in 1968 by President Lyndon Johnson. Congress also made it illegal to

President Lyndon B. Johnson signed the Civil Rights Act of 1964, banning segregation and prohibiting discrimination based on race, color, sex, nationality, or religion.

17

obstruct housing rights in any way due to a person's color, race, sex, nationality, or religion. In 1996, the Church Arson Prevention Act was passed, making it a crime to interfere with a person's religious practices, or to damage, deface, or destroy religious property.

The first states to pass hate crimes legislation were Oregon and Washington in 1981. As of 2018, forty-five states and the District of Columbia had laws criminalizing various types of hate crimes. Exceptions included Arkansas, Indiana, South Carolina, Wyoming, and Georgia, whose hate crime statute was struck down by the Georgia Supreme Court in 2004. Most states or large cities have hate crime task forces that work with community organizations as well as coordinate with the government.

The Story of James Byrd Jr.

On the evening of Saturday June 9, 1998, James Byrd Jr., a forty-nine-year-old black man, was walking home from his parents' house in a rural section of Texas near Jasper, a town known for Ku Klux Klan activity. James was accosted by three white men who took him into the woods and brutally beat him. One of the men slashed Byrd's throat, but not fatally, and another sprayed his face with black paint. The men then chained Byrd by the ankles to the back of their truck and dragged his body for three and a half miles down a country road.

Matthew Shepard
1976–1998

Peace

On Willett Drive in Laramie, Wyoming, there is a memorial bench for Matthew Shepard with the inscription, "He continues to make a difference. Peace be with him and all who sit here."

Byrd was conscious through most of the incident but passed out when his body hit a culvert, decapitating him. Byrd's head and arm were found in a ditch, nearly a mile away from his torso.

The perpetrators, Shawn A. Berry, Lawrence R. Brewer, and John W. King, were charged with murder for the heinous crime, which is considered to be one of the worst hate crimes in American history. The three men were roommates who had associations with the Klan. Brewer had intended to use this crime to promote his white supremacist organization. Brewer and King were sentenced to death, while Berry was sentenced to life in prison.

The Story of Matthew Shepard

On October 6, 1998, in Laramie, Wyoming, openly gay twenty-one-year-old student Matthew Shepard went to Fireside Lounge, a local pub. There he met Russell Henderson and Aaron McKinney, who lured him away from the bar. They took him to a rural area in Sherman Hills. Shepard was viciously beaten in the head with the butt of a .357 Smith & Wesson pistol. Henderson bound Shepard by the wrists with white clothesline, at McKinney's instruction. Taking his wallet and ID and shoes, they left him to die.

After a night of freezing temperature, Shepard was found eighteen hours later by a bicyclist. Shepard,

President Barack Obama expanded hate crimes laws in 2009 to protect victims of hate crimes based on sexual orientation, gender, gender identity, and disability.

though in a coma, held on to his life for four days in the intensive care unit. He was suffering from hypothermia and had a severely damaged brain stem and numerous bruises, lacerations, and welts. Shepard died just before 1:00 a.m. on October 12.

McKinney and Henderson were convicted of kidnapping and felony murders but they were not charged with a hate crime, despite the anti-gay slurs both men used throughout the trials. Each received two consecutive life terms. As a result of this horrific crime, activists called for federal legislation protecting LGBTQ people from violence.

Expansion of Hate Crimes Laws

On October 22, 2009, President Barack Obama signed the James Byrd Jr. and Matthew Shepard Hate Crimes Prevention Act. This measure expanded the Federal Hate Crime Law of 1969 to include protection for targets of hate crimes motivated by gender, sexual orientation, gender identity, or disability. It also provided both technical and monetary assistance to local, state, and tribal jurisdictions for the purpose of better investigating and prosecuting hate crimes.

Myths & FACTS

Myth: Hate crime laws are redundant because all crimes are hate crimes.

Fact: Hate crimes specifically target a group or a member of a group as a way to terrorize an entire community. They are motivated by hatred for that community. Naming hate crimes as hate crimes sheds light on the ways in which specific groups of people are marginalized and terrorized based on inherent aspects of their identities.

Myth: Hate crime laws restrict freedom of speech.

Fact: Speech, including offensive and hateful speech, is protected by the First Amendment. Hate crimes laws apply to criminal acts. If verbal or written speech includes a threat (for example, incentive to violence), that type of speech constitutes a crime and is not protected by the First Amendment.

(continued on the next page)

(continued from the previous page)

Myth: State statutes are redundant because there are federal hate crime laws.

Fact: Federal laws can have many limitations when applied at the state level. Hate crime statutes pertaining to specific states can enable prosecutions without the need for intervention by the federal government. Even the James Byrd Jr. and Matthew Shepard Hate Crimes Prevention Act has limitations at the state level.

Myth: Black Lives Matter is a militant black nationalist group.

Fact: Black Lives Matter exists to raise awareness of systemic racism in the United States and seek equal protection and treatment for all citizens, including black people. While there are black nationalist groups, Black Lives Matter is not one of them.

CHAPTER TWO

Causes and Effects of Hate Crimes

"H ate crimes are the scariest thing in the world," the singer Cher once noted, "because these people really believe what they're doing is right." People commit hate crimes for a number of reasons, including irrational fear and anger at people they perceive to be "other," the need to feel powerful, and a perverse sense that the person they are harming is inferior and somehow deserves to be attacked. While they can overlap at times, there are four core categories of people who commit hate crimes.

Thrill Seekers

These people are propelled to commit hate crimes by a craving for excitement coupled with the belief that their violent behavior will be applauded, or that society won't care about the victims. According to a 2008 study by Jack Levin and Jack McDevitt of Northeastern University, attackers of this nature are typically young, with 70 percent of these offenses including assaults that end with the victims being put in the hospital. Thrill seekers often go venturing out to find their victims.

Defenders

In hate crimes motivated by defensiveness, perpetrators usually act in response to a desire to defend their perceived space, such as a neighborhood, country, or workplace. These "defenders" justify their attacks by asserting they have warded off a threat. They are usually propelled to commit hate crimes by specific events, such as minorities moving to their neighborhood or allegedly encroaching upon jobs in their communities. These people typically have little to no remorse for their actions.

Protest can be a powerful way to make a statement. It also helps to energize and motivate people, because they realize they are not alone in their beliefs.

Retaliators

Retaliation hate crime acts are typically motivated by an idea of getting revenge for something. These perpetrators typically act alone and travel to the victim's space to carry out their hate crimes. Referred to as "eye-for-an-eye" attacks, this particular brand of hate crime spikes after acts of terrorism and disproportionately targets people who are perceived to be of Middle Eastern descent. After 9/11, hate crimes rose 1,600 percent against Arabs and Muslims, with attacks going from 28 in 2000 to 481 in 2011, according to FBI statistics.

Crusaders

Typically motivated by religious or racial bias and overlapping with terrorism, this type of hate crime is rare, but it's one of the deadliest. Perpetrators of this type of hate crime travel to sites

One example of a hate crime committed by a crusader is the shooting by Omar Mateen of forty-nine people at a gay nightclub in Orlando, Florida.

in the hopes of maximum carnage, and usually have websites, videos, or manifestos stating their views. Their agenda is all-out war against their perceived enemies. Some examples of crusaders include Omar Mateen, who massacred forty-nine people at a gay nightclub in Orlando, and Dylan Roof, who massacred nine black people in a Charleston church.

Bias Motivation Statistics

The FBI's Hate Crime Statistics program compiles data about hate crimes based on reports from law enforcement agencies across the country. According to the FBI's 2016 report, based on reporting from 1,776 agencies, there were 6,121 hate crime incidents, with 7,321 offenses. Of the 6,063 single-bias incidents, there were 7,227 single-bias hate crime offenses reported, with 7,509 victims, and 5,727 offenders. These hate crimes were motivated by the following biases:

- 58.5 percent—race/ethnicity/ancestry
- 21.3 percent—religious bias
- 16.9 percent—sexual-orientation bias
- 1.8 percent—gender-identity bias
- 1.1 percent—disability
- 0.5 percent—gender

In 2016, 4,229 single-bias hate crimes were reported that pertained to race, ethnicity, or ancestry. Those hate crimes were motivated by the following prejudices:

- 50.2 percent—anti-black or anti-African-American bias
- 20.7 percent—anti-white bias
- 10.6 percent—anti-Hispanic or anti-Latinx bias
- 5.8 percent—anti-other race/ethnicity/ancestry bias
- 4.2 percent—bias against groups consisting of more than one race
- 3.8 percent—anti-American Indian or Alaska Native bias
- 3.1 percent—anti-Asian bias
- 1.3 percent—anti-Arab bias
- 0.2 percent—anti-Native Hawaiian or other Pacific Islander bias

Impacts of Hate Crimes

In a speech at the Anti-Defamation League National Leadership Summit in 2014, former FBI Director James Comey noted that hate crimes, "strike at the heart of one's identity—they strike at our sense of self, our sense of belonging. The end result is loss—loss of trust, loss of dignity, and in the worst case, loss of life."

When a hate crime occurs, it doesn't just affect the victim. Any hate crime has a ripple effect, instilling fear in other members of the targeted community, making them afraid to go about their everyday lives. After the World Trade Center in New York City was attacked by Islamic extremists on September 11, 2001, hate crimes against Muslims increased from twenty-one to 481 reported incidents, and Muslims across the country became afraid for their safety.

In a Huffington Post article titled "20 Ways 9/11 Changed my Life as an (American) Muslim," Shawna Ayoub Ainslie wrote:

> *I was afraid to go outside. If I stayed inside, I couldn't mess up, except maybe with my words which I policed carefully. I couldn't speed, I couldn't frighten anyone.... I kept the headscarf I carried for prayer hidden in my purse instead of draped around my neck. I stopped reading the Qur'an between classes. I began pushing up my sleeves when in groups so people would not worry that I was conservative.*

I hoped they wouldn't even remember that I was Muslim.

PTSD

About seven or eight people in every one hundred will experience post-traumatic stress disorder (PTSD) at

PTSD can be hugely detrimental to sleep, causing nightmares, insomnia, and even hallucinations upon waking.

some point in their lives, according to the National Center for PTSD. Survivors of hate crimes or people whose communities or loved ones are targeted by hate crimes often suffer from PTSD in the wake of the crime. The likelihood of suffering from PTSD is increased when people have little to no support after a traumatic event. PTSD can be ongoing (chronic) or short term (acute) and people with this condition may have some or all of the following symptoms:

Reexperiencing

Reexperiencing symptoms manifest in the form of reoccurring nightmares, frightening thoughts, or flashbacks that cause people to feel like they're reliving the trauma. This is often accompanied by physical symptoms such as sweating or accelerated heart rate.

Avoidance

Avoidance means avoiding places, events, or activities that remind people of their traumatic experience, as well as avoiding thoughts related to the event. This is a common strategy for coping with trauma, but if it is done to an extreme degree, it can interfere with emotional recovery and healing.

Reactivity

Reactivity includes experiencing sudden, angry outbursts, being easily startled, having difficulty sleeping, or feeling "on edge" or tense.

Cognition & Mood Symptoms

Trauma can interfere with cognitive function and mood. Cognitive and mood symptoms can manifest in people losing interest in activities they used to enjoy, having negative thoughts about themselves or the world, having distorted feelings of blame, or having trouble remembering specific aspects of the traumatic event.

Mamie Till: A Mother's Choice that Changed History

As heinous and awful as hate crimes can be, they can sometimes be used as a learning point for society. Writer and civil rights activist Maya Angelou pointed out that, "History, despite its wrenching pain, cannot be unlived. But if faced with courage, need not be lived again." The murder of Emmett Till was one of the most gruesome and despicable hate crimes in American history. However, it can be viewed as a turning point in the civil rights movement.

In August 1955, Mamie Till sent her fourteen-year-old son, Emmett, down south to Mobley, Mississippi, to visit family. While he was out with family at a local store on August 24, the store owner's wife, Carolyn Bryant, accused Emmett of accosting her and asking her for a date. That night, the store owner, Roy Bryant, and his half-brother, J.W. Milam, went to Emmett's great uncle's home where he was staying, dragged him from bed, and took him out to a swamp where they beat him and then threw his body in the river. It took officials three days to find him, and when they did, the boy was unrecognizable, identified only by a ring on his finger, bearing his initials.

While Mississippi officials requested a quick burial, Mamie Till insisted on having what was left of her son brought home to be buried in Chicago. She then went a step further, allowing an open casket at the funeral. Thousands of people showed up to view the face of hatred in America. Emmett Till's battered face made the cover of magazines, holding up a mirror to the reality of racism in the South.

Mamie Till said, "I saw his tongue had been choked out, and it was lying down on his chin. This eye was out, and it was lying about mid-way the cheek. I discovered a hole. And I said, 'Well, was it necessary to shoot him?' I said I want the world to see this because, there is no way I could tell this story and give them the visual picture of what my son looked like."

Over 50,000 people came to Emmett Till's funeral to view his body. Mamie Till, his mother, wanted them to bear witness to the torture of her son.

Mamie's courage to show her dead son's face to the world sparked a movement. Though wounded to her soul, she stood up in the face of hatred. She even went to court to testify on behalf of her son.

Carolyn Bryant later admitted that she had lied about Emmett Till accosting her in the store. Shortly before her passing, she admitted that there was nothing Emmett had done that justified what happened to him. "Nothing that boy did could ever justify what happened to him," she told Duke University research scholar, historian, and author Timothy B. Tyson. And yet, back in 1955, she had testified that he had. Both men were acquitted, but years later they told *Look* magazine that they did in fact murder Emmett Till.

This brutal murder of this young black boy and his mother's choice to share her pain with the world reignited the civil rights movement. In fact, it was Emmett's face that made Rosa Parks refuse to give up her seat on that bus in Alabama. "I thought about Emmett Till," Parks said, "and I could not go back. My legs and feet were not hurting. That is a stereotype. I paid the same fare as others, and I felt violated. I was not going back."

CHAPTER THREE

Hate Groups in the United States

Contrary to popular belief, there are many organizations dedicated to extremist viewpoints or the idea that certain groups of people are inherently superior to others. According to the Southern Poverty Law Center (SPLC), there are 954 hate groups operating in the United States. Some of these groups operate statewide, without a specific hub or headquarters. The SPLC lists these 954 hate groups in the following categories: Anti-LGBT, Anti-Muslim, Black Nationalist, Christian Identity, General Hate, Hate Music, Holocaust Denial, Ku Klux Klan, Male Supremacy, Neo-Confederate, Neo-Nazi, Neo-Volkisch, Racist Skinhead, Radical Traditional Catholicism, and White Nationalist.

White Nationalism, White Supremacy, and the "Alt Right"

More than half of the hate crimes reported in the United States are motivated by racial bias, and more than half of those are the result of anti-black/anti-African American bias. The United States has a legacy of racism and systemic oppression of black people, with roots in slavery. While some people think that racism is a thing of the past, there are many white supremacist and white nationalist hate groups in existence. These include older groups like the Ku Klux Klan and neo-Nazis and newer groups that have come together under the "alt right" banner.

These groups share the ideology of white nationalism, which is the same thing as white supremacy. They desire an ethno-state—a nation run by white people for white people. They also believe that there is a correlation between IQ and race, and that black people have lower IQs than white people. Members of these groups have different goals. Some are

A group of white nationalists carry tiki torches and yell Nazi slogans like "blood and soil" and "Sieg heil!" at the University of Virginia in Charlottesville, Virginia, in August 2017.

focused on growing power politically while others are more interested in violence and inciting race war. Many of these groups are active beyond committing criminal acts. They hold rallies and marches, schedule speeches and meetings, and often publish content either online or in print. Some use Cloudflare and Bitcoin to fund their sites and activities.

Ku Klux Klan (KKK)

The most notorious white supremacist group in the United States, the KKK was formed after the Civil War in 1865 in Pulaski, Tennessee, by ex-Confederate officers, and had become a nationwide organization by the 1900s. A vigilante movement, it is known for targeting black Americans, and also openly discriminates against Jews, immigrants, and LGBTQ people. Active Klan groups have an estimated eight thousand members and span from New Jersey to Los Angeles. Subgroups include the Traditionalist American Knights and the Confederate White Knights.

Neo-Nazis

Neo-Nazi groups share a hatred of Jews and a love for Nazi Germany and Adolf Hitler. High profile neo-Nazi groups include the National Socialist Movement, the American Nazi Party, the National Alliance, and

Vanguard America. Members are estimated at 2,500 and neo-Nazis are thought to be active in thirty-two states. According to the Southern Poverty Law Center, links between European neo-Nazis and US neo-Nazis are strong.

With the help of social media platforms and sharing of memes, hate groups are not only mobilizing but growing.

Alt-Right

Alt-right, or alternative right, is a term that is often used to incorporate multiple far-right white nationalist groups, including the KKK and neo-Nazis. The term alt-right was popularized by white nationalist Richard Spencer around 2008. Spencer said "I like the term. It has an openness to it. And immediately understandable. We're coming from a new perspective." However, according to Oren Segal, director of the Anti-Defamation League Center on Extremism, it is really just "a new name for this old hatred." The alt-right movement is predominantly organized online, which makes the exact number of members hard to pinpoint.

White Supremacists Infiltrate Mainstream Politics in the Era of Trump

White nationalist groups saw a surge in activity during Donald Trump's 2016 presidential campaign, as a result of Trump's implicit support of white nationalist ideology. With the campaign slogan "Make America Great Again," Trump has been accused of using "dog-whistle" language to play to the racial resentment of his white supporters. According to German Lopez in Vox:

[Trump is] putting the idea of "law and order" above all else, even if it means a crackdown on minority communities. He's playing to people's "white fragility" and concerns about white heritage disappearing if Confederate statues come down. And he's pandering to concerns that undocumented immigrants are taking native-born (read: white) Americans' jobs.

For example, at a campaign rally in Nevada in 2016, Trump made the following remarks in response to a peaceful protester being ejected from the rally.

Oh, I love the old days, you know? You know what I hate? There's a guy totally disruptive, throwing punches, we're not allowed to punch back anymore. I love the old days. You know what they used to do guys like that when they were at a place like this? They'd be carried out on a stretcher, folks.

In response to this endorsement of violence, the crowd at the rally cheered.

Ian Haney-López, author of *Dog Whistle Politics: How Coded Racial Appeals Have Reinvented Racism and Wrecked the Middle Class,* made the following observation:

The dog whistle metaphor suggests that the dogs—the intended audience—hear the message clearly. That's wrong. The code is

Activist groups such as Black Lives Matter draw attention to the institutional nature of racism and its impacts on black communities across the United States.

designed to hide the actual dynamics from the target audience itself. It's code designed to allow people who are racially anxious and who are easily fired up with racial narratives to deny to themselves that it's race that's agitating them.

The target audience embraces the coded language "to protect themselves from the idea that they're being mobilized by racist appeals."

After Trump became president in 2016, white supremacists began to enter mainstream politics and organize more openly. After Trump appointed white nationalist Steve Bannon as the White House chief strategist, Adam Jentleson, a spokesman for then-Senate Democratic leader Harry Reid, pointed out, "It is easy to see why the KKK views Trump as their champion when Trump appoints one of the foremost peddlers of white supremacist themes and rhetoric as his top aide."

"Unite the Right" Rally in Charlottesville, Virginia

On August 11 and 12, 2017, white nationalists marched at the University of Virginia in Charlottesville, carrying tiki torches and shouting "blood and soil" and "white lives matter." The chant "blood and soil" is a right-wing nationalist slogan, meaning that "white blood" is connected to "American soil." It is in direct correlation to the German phrase "blut und boden," which was used by Hitler's Nazis. A good number of the protesters wore white supremacist pins. The use of tiki torches harks back to a dark corner of US history, when Ku Klux Klan rallies and lynch mobs would carry torches, utilizing them to intimidate and terrorize black people before lynching them.

This "Unite the Right" rally was organized by a number of far-right white nationalist groups to protest a vote to remove a statue of Robert E. Lee, a Confederate general, from a local public park. (The Confederate flag is predominantly associated with slavery and white supremacy.) Counterprotestors showed up and the scene became violent.

A memorial for Heather Heyer, thirty-two, who tragically died when a car plowed into counter-protesters at a "Unite the Right" rally in Charlottesville in 2017.

A state of emergency was declared in the city of Charlottesville and the county of Albemarle.

The violence culminated when James Alex Fields, one of the white nationalist protesters, drove his Dodge Challenger at high speeds into the crowd of anti-racist protesters. In addition to hitting people with his vehicle, he also rammed into a sedan, which then hit a minivan in front of it and more protestors. Ultimately, the crash ended up injuring nineteen people and killing thirty-two-year-old Heather Heyer.

Fields had been photographed earlier that day holding a symbol of Vanguard America. The manifesto for the group desires a government that "is based in natural law, and must not cater to the false notion of equality." Though the group has claimed no ties to Fields, it has strengthened his ties with neo-Nazis. Dating back to his high school years, Fields had taken a strong interest in World War II and the neo-Nazi movement.

President Trump did not condemn the actions of the white supremacists and neo-Nazis involved. Instead, he claimed that there was wrongdoing on both sides: "Well, I do think there's blame—yes, I think there's blame on both sides…. But you also had people that were very fine people, on both sides." Hate crimes and the ideologies that inspire them should be denounced immediately by public officials. The absence of this condemnation sends the message that hate crimes are acceptable and emboldens perpetrators of hate crimes.

Nazi and Holocaust Denier Becomes Republican Nominee

Arthur Jones, a seventy-year-old Holocaust denier and Nazi, became the official Republican nominee in the Third Congressional District of Illinois in March 2018. The Illinois Republican Party sent robocalls and campaign fliers to "stop Illinois Nazis," but to no avail. "Arthur Jones is not a real Republican—he is a Nazi whose disgusting, bigoted views have no place in our nation's discourse," said Illinois Republican Party chairman Tim Schneider, who urged voters to "skip over his name when they go to the polls." The Republican party planned to support an independent candidate in the general election later that year, and to give "real campaign dollars" in order to defeat Jones.

Jones has been active in the movement for white supremacy for years and is a former member of the American Nazi Party. As a college student at the University of Wisconsin, he attended meetings of the Nationalist Socialist student group and started a conservative campus newspaper. He went on to run

(continued on the next page)

(continued from the previous page)

for mayor of Milwaukee in 1976 while a member of the National Socialist White People's Party. Though Jones insisted that the "stuff about being a Nazi" was in his past, a page questioning the existence of the Holocaust remained on his campaign website. Jones has been known to have said that the Holocaust was "an international extortion racket" and "a greatly overblown non-event."

According to Jonathan Greenblatt, the chief executive officer of the Anti-Defamation League, Jones was one of several extremists who ran for public office in 2018. Some other examples include Joe Arpaio, a hardliner on immigration, and Paul Nehlen, an anti-Semite and self-described "pro-white" candidate. In the era of Trump, such extremists feel empowered to bring their abhorrent views into mainstream politics.

Living in a Culture of Hate: Being Prepared

Unfortunately, with so many active hate groups in the United States, hate crimes are a regular occurrence and many people encounter them at some point in their lives. However, there are things you can do to prepare yourself for the possibility of being a witness to or a victim of a hate crime.

Responding to hate crimes in a safe and helpful way takes preparation and practice. Whether the hate crime involves someone you know making a hateful comment or a stranger being attacked in the streets, such incidents are disturbing to witness. What would you say in this situation? What would you do? Coming up with a plan beforehand, practicing it by yourself, or role-playing with a friend will help you to feel more prepared if and when the time comes.

Many communities offer resources to prepare people to respond to hate crimes, whether they are the target of the hate crime or a bystander. There are classes in self-defense, bystander intervention, peer counseling, and deescalating a situation, among others. It's not easy to navigate an inflammatory situation, even when it only involves only words. That's why learning and training is essential.

One great way to be a helpful ally in the fight against hate crimes is to continue to educate and challenge yourself. There are some programs that offer courses in combating prejudice and changing the culture of hate.

Green Dot (https://alteristic.org/services/green -dot) offers training courses for adults and children as young as kindergarteners, covering topics such as active bystander practices to prevent teasing and

Taking a self-defense class can teach you to protect yourself and help you stay safe. Many community organizations offer free or low-cost classes.

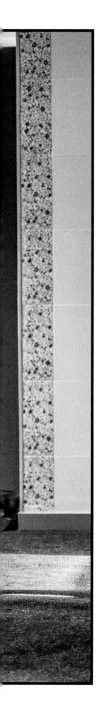

bullying. Green Dot can also certify attendees in Violence Prevention through its Green Dot Institute.

Hollaback! (https://www.ihollaback.org) is a global movement that focuses on ending harassment both in the streets and online and creating communities of resistance. It offers training programs including a leadership program for those who wish to lead in their own communities, as well as workshops that cover topics such as Building a Movement Around Ending Street Harassment Through Story Sharing, Bystander Intervention Techniques, and How to Build a Decentralized Movement That Matters.

In a country in which many hate groups are thriving with little to no condemnation from the president, it is vital that communities come together to stand up against hate groups and hate crimes and look out for each other. Education is an essential step in preparing to respond to hate crimes and to change the culture of hate.

CHAPTER FOUR

Responding to Hate Crimes

If you find yourself the victim of a hate crime, you should know that you are not alone, and that there are resources and advocates that can help you. Even if the hate crime doesn't involve physical violence, it can still be a traumatic experience. There is no right or wrong way to react, but there are a number of steps you can take to help yourself heal and to seek justice for the crime.

Acknowledge That It Happened

Sometimes, people who go through a traumatic experience use denial as a coping mechanism. By minimizing what has happened or acting as if the crime or incident isn't that big of a deal, people can avoid discussing it, reporting it, or taking any kind of action. But pretending that it didn't happen or that it didn't matter won't make it go away.

If you have suffered a loss or been the victim of a violent crime, your emotions may feel overwhelming sometimes. With the proper help, you can work to overcome them.

Coping with your own feelings and emotions begins with acknowledging to yourself that the hate crime really happened, and that it is serious.

Record It

As soon as you're able, it is important to record the details of what happened (when, where, and who), whether that be by video or audio recording or writing it down. Include as many details about the offender or offenders as possible, including gender, height, weight, approximate age, attire, and any other distinguishing features or characteristics that you can recall. It is also important to record if there were any threats made or slurs used.

Report It

It is important to file a police report so that there is an official record of what happened. You can do this by going to the police station in the city or town in which the incident occurred. Make sure that the officer files an incident report and assigns a case number, and that you receive a copy of the report. If there was a bias motivation to the incident, insist that the officer check the "hate crime/incident" or "hate/bias-motivation" box on the report. Also, make sure you receive the officer's name and badge number. This process may feel overwhelming. It's a good idea to bring a friend with you for support if possible.

Victims of hate crimes may be reluctant to report the crime for a number of reasons. Sometimes, recounting the events can cause them to relive the incident and make them feel embarrassed or ashamed. It is common for victims to blame themselves, especially when someone is attacked based on their identity or when a crime involves sexual violence.

Some victims may also fear retaliation from the perpetrator, or from others who support the perpetrator's actions, especially if the perpetrator is part of a group or organization that perpetuates hate. If the hate crime was motivated by homophobia or transphobia, the victim may be afraid of coming out publicly.

When it comes to interacting with the police, many victims of hate crimes may lack trust in the criminal justice system and fear that they won't be treated fairly and with dignity. This is a valid concern, particularly for people of color, LGBTQ individuals, people from low income communities, and survivors of sexual violence, who are often not treated with dignity or taken seriously by authorities. These fears may be heightened if the authorities themselves have been complicit in a hate crime or participated in one.

When reporting a hate crime to authorities, be sure to emphasize that it was a hate crime, so that it can be recorded as such.

It is important for hate crime survivors to know that they are not alone, and that even if the local authorities are not taking them seriously, there are advocates and organizations that can help. A good place to start is by checking out the websites Victim Connect (www.VictimConnect.org) and Hate Crime Help (www.HateCrimeHelp.com), which is also an app, for further resources.

In general, hate crimes are underreported. When people report hate crimes, they contribute to the data that illustrates the magnitude of the problem of hate crimes in the United States. When authorities have this data, it puts more pressure on them to implement policies and laws that help to prevent and prosecute hate crimes.

Reporting Online Hate

Even though many people use fake profiles when they harass and threaten people online, there are still things you can do to report such intimidating behavior. All social media platforms have codes of conduct. Representatives of Facebook, YouTube, Twitter, and Microsoft have signed a code of conduct formulated by the European Commission, agreeing to counter illegal hate speech online, and fight against its spread. This agreement includes reviewing reports of illegal hate speech on their platforms within a twenty-four-hour period, and either disabling access or removing the profiles altogether. The code of conduct defines this type of illegal hate speech as "all conduct publicly inciting to violence or hatred directed against a group of persons or a member of such a group defined by reference to race, color, religion, descent or national or ethnic origin."

Reach Out for Support

When you are recovering from a hate crime, having support can be crucial. Support can be a friend, a family member, a teacher, or anyone who makes you feel safe. You may also want to talk to a school counselor or therapist who can help you sort through your feelings and help you make sense of things. Support can also take the form of groups or support services. The Center for Anti-Violence Education is a useful resource to help you find a support organization in your area.

Talking things through is part of the healing process. Professionals are trained to help, but even a sympathetic friend can make you feel both heard and supported.

Coping with Trauma and PTSD

If you or a loved one has suffered a traumatic incident, there are a number of things you can do to avoid getting PTSD, or to heal from PTSD. These include:

- Reaching out to a sympathetic friend who will listen as you talk through your feelings, finding a therapist, or joining a support group.
- Seeing a medical professional to get an official diagnosis and get advice about treatment. Your doctor may prescribe medication to help you cope with PTSD.
- Exercising regularly in a manner you enjoy to help reduce stress and help boost your mood.
- Getting enough sleep.
- Making time to do things you enjoy or spend time with people you find comforting.
- Setting boundaries for what you feel comfortable doing or talking out. Don't feel obliged to share your feelings or story with someone if you don't want to.
- Breaking down larger tasks into smaller tasks to make them more manageable, if you feel overwhelmed.

Trauma is common, but with the proper care and treatment, you can get through it and begin to enjoy your life again. The sooner you get help, the sooner you'll have access to coping tools that will assuage your symptoms and help you to heal. If you don't get treatment, it is likely that your symptoms will continue and may even get worse. Additionally, while symptoms such as nightmares may disappear, it is possible that they may return, particularly in the event of another stressful or traumatic event.

If you or someone you know is suffering from PTSD, you can find lots of helpful information on the National Center for PTSD's website (https://www.ptsd .va.gov) or the National Institute of Mental Health's website (https://www.nimh.nih.gov/health/find-help /index.shtml).

Working with Hate Crime Victims

If you know someone who has been the victim of a hate crime, there are a few things you can do to support that person and help him take appropriate next steps.

- Help the victim feel safe and in control of the situation. An example of this would be creating a safety plan designed around her triggers.

(continued on the next page)

(continued from the previous page)

- Let him know you are available for discussion, but do not pressure the victim. Allow him to come to you in his own time.
- Assist the victim in receiving medical or mental health care. Visit MentalHealth.gov for help in finding treatment.
- Make sure the survivor knows that she has legal rights, including the right to be treated with dignity and respect, the right to be informed about her rights, the right to protection, the right to apply for compensation (including medical and counseling expenses), the right to restitution from the offender, the right to prompt return of personal property, the right to a speedy trial, and the right to the enforcement of victims' rights. Visit VictimsOfCrime.org for more information.
- Help the victim in reporting the crime to authorities and offer to accompany him.
- Access your networks to find appropriate resources for support.
- Help the victim prepare for meetings or interviews regarding the hate crime, including speaking with media. This includes helping her know what to bring and what to wear, preparing her responses to questions, and paying attention to nonverbal communication.

Bystander Intervention

In any situation involving hate, you need to know how to keep yourself safe, as well as helping others. Caution is just as important as courage. If you are witnessing a violent hate crime, or a hate crime that seems like it could become violent, don't insert yourself into the situation. Instead, get help as quickly as possible by calling 911.

There are a few things you can do to intervene if it feels safe to do so—that is, if the threat level is low, meaning there's no danger of physical harm. If somebody is being verbally harassed, one way for bystanders to help while avoiding confrontation is to go up to the person being harassed and strike up a friendly conversation with her, ignoring the perpetrator. Compliment a piece of her clothing, talk about the weather, or ask for directions. Engage the person in small talk while ignoring the perpetrator. Often, the perpetrator will be thrown off and go away. Still, be sure not to turn your back on the perpetrator. Ignore him, but be on guard and be sure you can see him at all times.

Advice for Allies

If you know someone who has been affected by a hate crime, there are a few ways you can learn to be a supportive ally. Being an ally is not just something you do once, but an ongoing process of listening, supporting, and becoming aware of how hate crimes work. If you are a person with privilege, you may have a lot of work to do to educate yourself about how systemic oppression works.

Listen First

Sometimes, it's hard to focus on another person speaking without injecting your own thoughts and feelings into the situation. When someone you know has gone through a traumatic experience, such as being the victim of a hate crime, it's important that you practice being an active listener. This means giving the person your undivided attention, refraining from judgment, and providing support. Active listening improves your understanding of the situation, as you are listening attentively instead of thinking about what you want the person to do or say.

Educate Yourself

Listening is important, but so is independent study. There are many resources available to

Group therapy can be beneficial, particularly for those who have experienced a type of loss. Being a part of a group like this can help you realize that you aren't alone.

help you learn about oppression, PTSD, and systemic oppression—YouTube videos, books, blogs, and more. The more you learn, the more you will grow, and that growth will help you respond in a helpful way. Asking questions of friends who are victimized by hate crimes can be OK sometimes, but if your friend has experienced a traumatic event, she may not have the emotional capacity to explain everything to you, so it is a good idea to take responsibility for educating yourself.

Remember, It's Not About You

If you are a person with privilege, it's possible you may be given the space to speak for others because of your race or gender. It's important, however, to turn that platform over to the those who are most marginalized and most impacted by hate crimes. Remember, this isn't about strengthening your voice or your career. It's about providing true support.

Know That You'll Make Mistakes, and That's Okay

Everybody makes mistakes. When you get something wrong, listen, learn, and apologize. Hold yourself accountable and be earnest with your intent. Move forward the right way. As the late great Maya Angelou

"Hate, it has caused a lot of problems in the world, but has not solved one yet." —Maya Angelou, 1948–2014

said, "Do the best you can until you know better. Then when you know better, do better."

Have the Social Courage to Educate Others

If you are a person with privilege, one of the most helpful things you can do is to talk to other people like you who may be uninformed about how prejudice works. This could be a relative, a friend, or a neighbor who is reluctant to believe that racism or homophobia really exist, but who may be more likely to listen to someone they know, or someone who's "like them." Engaging others in the struggle for equality is a powerful thing to do.

Have Compassion and Give Space

Compassion is key, and sometimes the best form of compassion is giving someone the space he or she needs. Survivors of hate crimes need the space to process what has happened to them and figure out what they want the next step to be. You can continue to be a comforting presence by letting people know that you're there for them, that you see their fear, and that you are bearing witness to what has occurred. To have a witness is to have validation, which helps people to heal and rebuild strength.

Take Action

In the age of social media, it's easy to post on Facebook or Twitter, or respond to an online comment and feel a sense of accomplishment. As great as it is to put positivity out on the internet or combat online trolls, these social media posts often don't accomplish much. Oftentimes, given the bias people have in choosing their online friends, social media interactions become an echo chamber, with everyone preaching to their own respective choirs.

However, there are measures you can take to help create real change in your community. You can organize a peaceful rally in your community to respond to hate crimes. You can call or email your elected officials, demanding that they take specific action in response to a hate crime, and you can encourage others to do the same. This can be as simple as sharing contact info for the elected official and providing a stock letter that your friends and contacts can customize and send. You can also join a local community group or a national organization, such as the ACLU, that organizes around hate crime issues.

CHAPTER FIVE

Changing the Culture of Hate

Former president of South Africa Nelson Mandela once noted, "No one is born hating another person because of the color of his skin, or his background, or his religion. People must learn to hate, and if they can learn to hate, they can be taught to love, for love comes more naturally to the human heart than its opposite." While many people are set in their ways when it comes to how they perceive others, the possibility to change is within everyone. Sometimes, it's just a matter of bringing it out in the right way or, in some instances, by the right person.

Building Bridges

Preventing hate crimes begins with understanding why hate crimes happen to begin with, which

"The time for the healing of the wounds has come. The moment to bridge the chasms that divide us has come."
—Nelson Mandela, 1918–2013

requires examining bias in our own communities. Hatred develops when people learn to fear people they perceive as "other." One great way to address this problem is by bridging the gap between people who are different from each other.

In 2017, Cheryle Moses, the founder of Urban Mediamakers, organized a two-hour networking event in Lawrenceville, Georgia, where nonblack people could come and meet and break bread with black people. Moses was inspired by a 2013 study by the Public Religion Research Institutes that stated that 75 percent of white people in the United States don't have any non-white friends, and that 65 percent of black people don't have white friends. Moses told the *Washington Post*:

> *As a black person, I deal with racism every day. It's a part of life. Nowadays, I have become more fearful. I have never been afraid when it comes to race, but now I am. And I don't think I'm*

One great way to overcome the culture of hate is to build bridges across culture by reaching out to people who are different from you.

alone. I want to do my part to change things…. The only way to change the divisiveness that's going on is to be one-on-one with people. Policy won't change things, but forming relationships will.

Intolerance and hate usually stem from fear of the unknown. When a bigoted person actually gets to know someone from another group, his ignorance and fear often dissipates. Making connections with people who are different from you is a great step in eliminating the kind of ignorance that leads to hate. Simply making human connections can save lives.

Speaking Up for Yourself and Others

It can be hard to stand up to prejudice when everyone around you is going along with it. But having the moral and social courage to stand up for what you believe in can change the hearts and minds of people around you. If you witness someone being harassed and nobody is doing anything to intervene, it can be hard to know how to respond.

Not every example of hate is overt or dangerous. It could be something as simple as listening to a relative expressing his bigotry over Thanksgiving dinner. Many people would be inclined to brush it off as "just Uncle Mike being Uncle Mike." In reality, this type of bigotry, when it goes unchecked, perpetuates the culture of hate. If you don't say anything, others at the table may believe it's OK. If there are children listening, they may go out and make prejudicial statements because that's what they heard Uncle Mike say, and nobody contradicted him. If you have the courage to stand up to bigotry, however incidental it may seem, you are playing a role in changing the culture of hate.

Community Organizing

There are a number of community organizations and national NGOs that do important work to prevent hate crimes, provide support for victims, and raise awareness about the culture of hate. If you want to get involved on a wider scale in the fight to end hate crimes, you may consider joining one of these organizations. One example is OCA—Asian Pacific American Advocates, which is "dedicated to advancing the social, political and economic well-being of Asian Americans and Pacific Islanders." This organization has published a range of literature regarding hate crimes, including information about the importance of building a network for prevention.

Just because you are a student doesn't mean you don't have the power to create change. In fact, young people are often at the forefront of activist movements. In March 2018, twenty colleges across America participated in the Anti-Defamation League's "Innovate Against Hate" campaign. In order to combat extremism and hate, they came up with social media

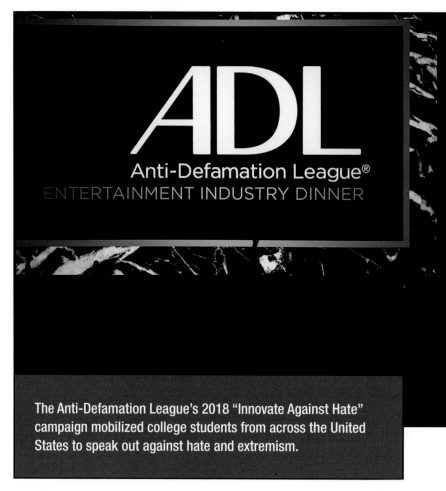

The Anti-Defamation League's 2018 "Innovate Against Hate" campaign mobilized college students from across the United States to speak out against hate and extremism.

marketing campaigns and digital initiatives to push for equality, fairness, and inclusion.

When a group of people from different backgrounds come together to speak out about hate crimes, they create a safer space for survivors of hate crimes to come forward and report hate crimes. These survivors know that they have support in their communities. Even if they are afraid that their local authorities may not treat them with dignity,

they know that there are people who will listen and understand what they're going through.

When a community pulls together in an official capacity to denounce hate publicly, it sends a message to police and government officials that hateful behavior will not be tolerated. This may spur local authorities and elected officials to take hate crimes more seriously, which could involve providing trainings for law enforcement officers, providing increased assistance for victims of hate crimes, and changing laws to protect citizens from hate crimes.

The "Take Action" Task List

Most people have busy lives and it is hard to find time to keep working toward change when there are so many other things to do. By making yourself a "take action" task list and keeping it in a place where you will see if often, you can keep yourself accountable as you go about your daily life. Here are some examples of items for your task list.

- Seek information to make yourself more aware of why hate crimes happen, and more empathetic to people who are different from you in various ways.
- Reflect on your past behaviors, both actions and words, and think about how they may have contributed, combated, or allowed you to be complicit with attitudes and ideologies of hate.
- Refuse to accept openly prejudicial or bigoted language around you, even if in jest, and even if it's from a friend or family member.
- Have the social (and social media) courage to call out inaccuracies and untruths that can be harmful to the image and treatment of any group of people.

- Vote with conscience and knowledge, choosing candidates who take a firm stance against racism, sexism, ableism, ageism, xenophobia, homophobia, transphobia, or any other kind of bias that isolates, diminishes, or harms a group of people.
- Evaluate your buying habits to avoid supporting any company or agency that promotes harm or hate, and end affiliations with organizations that do.
- Investigate and learn about a culture that's different from your own.

Changing the Culture in Schools

Schools and other educational facilities make the ideal places for people to learn to examine their own biases when they are young, but many schools are not equipped with the resources to provide this type of anti-bias education. For educational professionals or others who want to change the culture of schools, there are a number of great resources out there. These include ASCD.org's *Educational Leadership* journal and the websites 7 Mindsets (7Mindsets.com) and Education Week (edweek.org).

Former teacher and college professor Jane Elliott created the controversial "Blue Eyes/Brown Eyes" exercise in response to the assassination of Dr. Martin Luther King Jr. The exercise aims to teach participants the experience of being a minority. Elliott offers lectures, workshops, and videos about her teachings and the importance of combating racism.

Finding a Role Model

Role models can be a source of inspiration and help provide a blueprint for how you want to live your life and make the world a better place. Your role model could be a historical figure like Harriet Tubman, who escaped from slavery then returned many times to the deep South to help others escape. She worked as a spy for the Union, and later became a well-known speaker and an advocate for African American rights and the rights of black women. Or it could be a modern-day hero such as Malala Yousafzai, the Pakistani schoolgirl who fought for the right to

Malala Yousafzai is an inspiration. Not only is she a girls' rights activist, but she's also a Nobel Peace Prize winner.

education for girls, despite receiving threats from the Taliban. After surviving a gunshot to the head by the Taliban, Yousafzai became a global advocate for women's rights, the right to education, and human rights, all before her twenty-first birthday. Your role model doesn't have to be someone famous though. It could be someone in your family or community who is courageous and takes a stand. Keeping this person in your mind when you feel hopeless or helpless can give you the strength to continue standing up for what you believe in.

Confronting Hatred Head-On

It is never advisable to confront an angry mob. However, there are a few surprising stories of people facing members of hate groups head-on and managing to persuade them to question or even reconsider their beliefs and actions.

The Story of Daryl Davis

Daryl Davis, an African American blues musician from Chicago, was the only black man in a country band. Back in 1983 after a set in Frederick, Maryland, a white man in the audience approached him and complimented him on his musical skills. As the two men engaged in further conversation over a drink, the man told Davis that he had never had a drink with or even talked to a black person before. When Davis asked him why not, the man explained simply that he was a member of the Ku Klux Klan, and he produced his Klan card. They exchanged numbers and the two became unlikely friends. But that was only the beginning.

Having grown up abroad, Davis became fascinated with racism and the motivation of racists. By befriending Klan members, he dismantled the Klan in Maryland, one by one, collecting robes and hoods over a period of three decades. As of August 2017, Daryl Davis had persuaded two hundred Ku Klux Klan members to give up their robes, according to Davis in an interview on NPR's *All Things Considered*.

Davis offered the following logic for why he chooses to befriend KKK members:

> *If you have an adversary with an opposing point of view, give that person a platform. Allow them to air that point of view, regardless of how extreme it may be.... You challenge them. But you don't challenge them rudely or violently. You do it politely and intelligently. And when you do things that way, chances are they will reciprocate and give you a platform.... There are a lot of*

well-meaning white liberals. And a lot of well-meaning black liberals. But [...] when all they do is sit around and preach to the choir, it does absolutely no good. If you're not racist, it doesn't do any good for me to meet with you and sit around and talk about how bad racism is.

The Story of Ali Ghouri

In March of 2017, a group of anti-Muslim activists calling themselves BAIR (Bureau of American Islamic Relations) protested outside a mosque in Richardson, Texas, accusing the mosque's members of supporting terrorists. They were armed with assault rifles and "Stop the Islamization of America" signs. Ali Ghouri, a member of the mosque, faced the protesters head-on. He told them, "I have a weapon. You have a weapon. I'm not scared of you."

On the afternoon of the protest, Ghouri invited David Wright, one

Speaking out publicly about injustice is one way to combat the culture of hate. Others include having honest conversations with people who have different values from you.

of the BAIR protesters, to lunch to talk about their differing issues. Wright was going to say no until a local reporter mentioned that he'd want to go as well to cover the story. The appeal of publicity lead to Wright saying yes.

They ended up talking for two hours over halal sandwiches, with Ghouri explaining that his religion was peaceful, and that donations were vetted by the mosque's leadership to make sure they went to the right people. Though Wright was skeptical, Ghouri felt hopeful. "I think I saw a little bit in him that he did not want to hate Muslims," Ghouri told Robert Samuels in an interview for the *Washington Post*. Ghouri felt it was possible that, over time, Wright might change his beliefs.

Three months later, the two men arranged to meet again to continue their conversation. This time they met at Dairy Queen. Ghouri arrived with his friend Tameem Budri and Wright brought a fellow BAIR member, Christopher Gambino, to accompany him. The four men sat at a table in the Dairy Queen, ordered food, and talked.

During the discussion, Ghouri asked, "Why do you have to feel superior? Are we forcing them [Christians] to speak another language or do another thing? No. You do whatever you want to do." To this, Gambino replied that the presence of Muslims just made some people feel uncomfortable.

"The best way to handle that is to get to know each other," Ghouri said. "Otherwise, this cycle of hate is going to continue and the fear we have of each other will never go away."

The conversation continued for three hours and ended with the men smoking cigarettes together in the parking lot. Budri told Wright and Gambino that he had respect for them. In response, Gambino said that Budri had a lot of integrity, and he admitted that he had learned a lot from the conversation.

Before their meeting came to a close, Wright told the group that he would no longer protest in front of any mosque.

Hope for the Future

Dr. Martin Luther King Jr. once said, "Don't ever let anyone pull you so low as to hate them… We must have compassion and understanding for those who hate us… We stand in life at midnight; we are always on the threshold of a new dawn."

When it comes to altering the culture of hate, people must be willing to engage, and to have uncomfortable conversations. When it comes to fighting hatred, there is a lot of work to do. The endgame should be not only to protect one another, but to change the culture of hate itself. This depends on individuals working to educate themselves and

Though best remembered for his "I Have a Dream" speech, Dr. Martin Luther King Jr. was a prolific man whose calls for progress still inspire activists decades later.

the people around them. It also means continuing to stand up for one another.

President Barack Obama once said:

I will never forget that the only reason I'm standing here today is because somebody, somewhere, stood up for me when it was risky. Stood up when it was hard. Stood up when it wasn't popular. And because that somebody stood up, a few more stood up. And then a few thousand stood up. And then a few million stood up. And standing up, with courage and clear purpose, they somehow managed to change the world.

10 Great Questions to Ask a Representative at a Social Justice Organization

1. How can I call out bigoted speech by friends and family without alienating people?

2. Where should I go to report this hate crime?

3. If I witness a hate crime, how can I help the victim without putting myself in danger?

4. What should I do if I witness or hear about a hate crime but the victim doesn't want to report it?

5. If I hear a child spouting hateful language, what should I do?

6. Someone close to me supports political figures and ideologies that I find offensive. Do I need to distance myself from him?

7. Someone I know is racist/sexist/homophobic. How can I get her to change her views?

8. I was a victim of a hate crime and I want to share my story with the public. What is the best way to do that?

9. What is the proper response if I see symbols of hate (noose, swastika, written racial slurs, etc.) in a public place?

10. What can I do on a local level to get involved with the fight against hate crimes?

Glossary

activist A person who campaigns to bring about political or social change.

ally A person or organization that supports or helps another person or group of people.

anti-Semite A person who is prejudiced against Jews.

bias The favoring of a specific person, group, or thing over another, usually in a way considered to be unfair.

civil liberties Individual rights in regard to freedom of speech and action that are protected from unjust government interference by the law.

discrimination The unjust or prejudicial treatment of different categories of people or things, especially on the grounds of race, age, or sex.

diversity A variety or range of people from different backgrounds, races, cultures, religions, genders, nationalities, etc.

hate crime A crime motivated by prejudice against a person or group of people based on their identify. Examples include physical assault, criminal damage, sexual assault, or murder.

hate incident An occurrence or action motivated by prejudice against a person or group of people based on their identify. Examples include verbal abuse, harassment, intimidation or bullying, threats of violence, abusive phone calls, hate mail, online abuse, property damage, or circulating discriminatory literature.

hostility To act in an antagonistic, combative, or unfriendly manner toward a person or people.

ideology The ideas and school of thought underpinning a group or institution.

intolerance Unwillingness to accept views, beliefs, or behavior that differ from one's own.

lacerations A deep cut or tear in the skin or flesh.

minority A group of people that differ from the dominant group in some way (such as race or religion) and are often discriminated against as a result of that difference.

nationalist A person who believes that his country is superior to others.

perpetrator A person who carries out a harmful act.

prejudice A negative judgment made about a person or group of people based on preconceived opinions, rather than reason or experience.

prevention The action of stopping something from happening or arising.

privilege A special right, advantage, or immunity granted or available only to a particular person or group of people.

PTSD Post-traumatic stress disorder; a condition of ongoing mental and emotional stress occurring as a result of a traumatic event.

social courage Not giving in to societal and social pressures while doing what is right.

slur A derogatory or insulting term applied to a particular group of people.

supremacist A person who believes that his race is inherently superior to other races and should have power over other races.

stereotype A simplistic and oftentimes erroneous view or image of a group of people that is widely accepted by society.

vandalism Deliberate destruction of or damage to public or private property.

For More Information

Alberta Hate Crimes Committee (AHCC)
Website: http://www.albertahatecrimes.org
Email: AlbertaHateCrimes@gmail.com
Twitter: @ABHateCrime
Alberta Hate Crimes Committee works to promote
   awareness about hate crimes and hate incidents,
   addresses the needs of victims, enhances
   government and community responses, and
   offers workshops in areas such as how to start a
   dialogue in your community.

ALTERISTIC
7955 Cameron Brown Court
Springfield, VA 22153
(571) 319-0354
Website: https://alteristic.org
Facebook: @alteristic
Twitter and Instagram: @AlteristicOrg
Alteristic offers programs and classes for adults
   and children. The organization's Green Dot
   program teaches active bystander practices to
   prevent bullying and can provide certification
   in Violence Prevention.

DoSomething.org
Website: https://www.dosomething.org
(917) 627-8910
Facebook, Twitter, and Instagram: @dosomething

DoSomething.org is a global movement that works with youth to make positive change in their communities, schools, and online. The organization is active across the United States and in over 131 countries.

hollaback!
Website: https://www.ihollaback.org
Facebook, Twitter, and Instagram: @ihollaback
Hollaback is a global movement to end harassment. Hollaback offers programs to train youth to become community leaders, helping to create communities of resistance, generate public conversation, and create strategies to ensure equality in public spaces.

National Center for PTSD
US Department of Veterans Affairs
810 Vermont Avenue, NW
Washington, DC 20420
Website: https://www.ptsd.va.gov
(802) 296-6300
Facebook: @VAPTSD
Twitter: @VA_PTSD_Info
YouTube: Veterans Health Administration
The National Center for PTSD is dedicated to research and education on PTSD and trauma.

RAINN & National Sexual Assault Hotline
(800) 656-HOPE (4673)
Website: https://www.rainn.org
Facebook: @RAINN01
Twitter and Instagram: @RAINN
RAINN is the largest US organization combating
    sexual violence through education and hotlines.
    The organization coordinates with local sexual
    assault partners and the Department of Defense.

The Trevor Project
PO Box 69232
West Hollywood, CA 90069
(866) 488-7386
Website: https://www.thetrevorproject.org
Facebook: @TheTrevorProject
Twitter and Instagram: @TrevorProject
The Trevor Project is a crisis intervention
    nonprofit specifically addressing the needs of
    LGBTQ young people.

VictimsInfo.ca
Website: http://www.victimsinfo.ca
(800) 563-0808
Victims Info provides online resources for both
    victims and witness of crimes in British
    Columbia, Canada.

For Further Reading

Abdel-Fattah, Randa. *Does My Head Look Big in This?* London, England: Scholastic Paperbacks, 2014.

Abramovitz, Melissa. *Hate Crimes in America.* Minneapolis, MN: Essential Library, 2017.

Alexie, Sherman. *The Absolutely True Diary of a Part-time Indian.* New York, NY: Little Brown Books for Young Readers, 2007.

Davidson, Danica. *Everything You Need to Know About Hate Crimes.* New York, NY: Rosen Young Adult, 2018.

De Grazia, Don. *American Skin: A Novel.* New York, NY: Scribner Paperback Fiction, 2000.

Irving, Debby. *Waking Up White: And Finding Myself in the Story of Race.* Cambridge, MA: Elephant Room Press, 2014.

Linn, Laurent. *Draw the Line.* New York, NY: Margaret K. McElderry Books, 2017.

Mitchell, Don. *The Freedom Summer Murders.* New York, NY: Scholastic Press, 2014.

Myracle, Lauren. *Shine.* New York, NY: Amulet Books, 2011.

Parker Rhodes, Jewell. *Ghost Boys.* New York, NY: Little Brown Books for Young Readers, 2018.

Rankine, Claudia. *Citizen: An American Lyric.* Minneapolis, MN: Graywolf Press, 2014.

Reynolds, Jason, and Brendan Kiely. *All American Boys.* New York, NY: Atheneum, 2017.

Slater, Dashka. *The 57 Bus: A True Story of Two Teenagers and the Crime That Changed Their Lives*. New York, NY: Farrar, Straus and Giroux, 2017.

Stone, Nic. *Dear Martin*. New York, NY: Crown Books for Young Readers, 2017.

Thomas, Angie. *The Hate U Give*. New York, NY: Harper Collins Publishers, 2017.

Till-Mobley, Mamie. *Death of Innocence: The Story of the Hate Crime That Changed America*. New York, NY: Random House, 2011.

Bibliography

British Counsel. "Dealing with Hate Crime." UK Life. Retrieved April 4, 2018. http://esol .britishcouncil.org/content/learners/uk-life /be-safe-uk/dealing-hate-crime.

Brown, Dwane. "How One Man Convinced 200 Ku Klux Klan Members to Give Up Their Robes." NPR. August 20, 2017. https://www .npr.org/2017/08/20/544861933/how-one -man-convinced-200-ku-klux-klan-members -to-give-up-their-robes.

Burke, Daniel. "The Four Reasons People Commit Hate Crimes." CNN. June 12, 2017. https:// www.cnn.com/2017/06/02/us/who-commits -hate-crimes/index.html.

Craig-Henderson, Kellina, and L. Ren Sloan. "After the Hate: Helping Psychologists Help Victims of Racist Hate Crime." Research Gate. May 2006. https://www.researchgate .net/publication/229767413_After_the_Hate _Helping_Psychologists_Help_Victims_of _Racist_Hate_Crime.

Davidson. "Difference Between a Hate Crime and a Bias Incident." Student Life. https://www .davidson.edu/student-life/multicultural-life /hate-crime-and-bias-incidents.

Essex Victims' Gateway. "Hate Crime." Coping with Crime. Retrieved April 4, 2018. https://www .essexvictimsgateway.org.

Gurman, Sadie, and Russell Contreras. "Report: More Than Half of Hate Crimes in US Go Unreported." *Chicago Tribune.* June 29, 2017. http://www.chicagotribune.com/news /nationworld/ct-hate-crimes-unreported -20170628-story.html.

International Association of Chiefs of Police. "Responding to Hate Crimes: A Police Officer's Guide to Investigation and Prevention." TheIACP.org. Retrieved April 4, 2018. http:// www.theiacp.org/ViewResult?SearchID=123.

Jacobson, Louis. "Are There White Nationalists in The White House?" Politifact. August 15, 2017. http://www.politifact.com/truth-o -meter/article/2017/aug/15/are-there-white -nationalists-white-house/.

Kaur, Lakhpreet. "Here's Why Hate Crimes Happen." Huffington Post, September 14, 2015. https:// www.huffingtonpost.com/lakhpreet-kaur/why -do-hate-crimes-happen_b_8127918.html.

National Center for Transgender Equality. "Responding to Hate Crimes: A Community Resource Manual." TransEquality.org. July 2009. https://transequality.org/sites/default/files /docs/resources/NCTE_Hate_Crimes _Manual.pdf.

Northeastern Illinois University. "Instructions for Responding to Hate Crimes." Retrieved April 4,

2018. http://neiu.edu/universitylife/sites/neiu .edu.universitylife/files/documents/lvalenti /InstructionsforRespondingtoHateCrimes.pdf.

Oberst, Skyler. "How to Respond to Hate Crimes." Spokane Favs. Retrieved April 4, 2018. https:// spokanefavs.com/how-to-respond-to-hate -crimes/.

Organization for Security and Cooperation in Europe. "Preventing and Responding to Hate Crimes." OSCE.org. Retrieved April 4, 2018. http://www .osce.org/odihr/39821?download=true.

Philips, Suzanne. "How Do We Cope with Hate Crimes? Three Considerations." Psych Central. Retrieved April 4, 2018. https://blogs .psychcentral.com/healing-together/2016/06 /how-do-we-cope-with-hate-crimes-three -considerations/.

Samuels, Robert. "A Showdown over Sharia: Two groups of men, deeply suspicious of each other, meet at a Dairy Queen." *The Washington Post*. September 22, 2017. https://www .washingtonpost.com.

Southern Poverty Law Center. "Ten Ways to Fight Hate: A Community Response Guide." SPLCenter.org, August 14, 2017. https://www .splcenter.org/20170814/ten-ways-fight-hate -community-response-guide.

Sullivan, John, et al. "Nationwide, Police Shot and Killed Nearly 1000 People in 2017." *The Washington Post.* January 6, 2018. https://www.washingtonpost.com.

UK Race and Europe Network. "Dealing with Hate Crime: A Guide for Victims and NGOs Helping Victims" UKREN.org. March 2017. http://www.ukren.org/uploads/Dealing%20with%20hate%20crime.pdf.

You & Co. "What Is Hate Crime?" Coping with The Effects of Crime Together. Retrieved April 4, 2018. https://www.youandco.org.uk/crime-info/what-hate-crime.

Index

A

abusive language, 10
advice for allies, 67–68, 70, 72
  education, 68, 70, 72
  have compassion, 72
  listen, 68
  take action, 73
"alt right," 40, 44
Angelou, Maya, 35, 70
Anti-Defamation League, 44, 52, 79
  National Leadership Summit (2014), 32
anti-Semite, 52

B

Bannon, Steve, 47
bias, 13, 14, 15, 28, 30, 31, 40, 58, 73, 76, 83
bias motivation statistics, 30–31
Black Lives Matter, 24
Byrd Jr., James, 14, 18, 20, 22, 24
bystander intervention, 53, 55, 67

C

Center for Anti-Violence Education, 63
changing culture of hate, 74–93
  building bridges, 74, 76, 78
  community organizing, 79–81
  find role model, 84
  in schools, 83–84
  speaking up, 78–79
Chapa, Jason and Victoria, 4–6
Church Arson Prevention Act (1996), 18
civil liberties, 8
Civil Rights Act (1964), 16
civil rights movement, 35, 38
confronting hatred, 86
  Davis, Daryl, 86–88
  Ghouri, Ali, 88, 90–91

D

disability, 6, 8, 10, 22, 31

E

ethno-state, 40

F

Federal Bureau of Investigation (FBI), 6,

8, 15, 16, 28, 30, 32
Federal Hate Crimes
    Prevention Act (1969),
    16, 22
freedom of speech, 8, 23

G

gender, 8, 10, 12, 22, 31,
    58, 70
gender-bias crimes,
    13–14
gender identity, 6, 22, 31
genocide, 16
Green Dot, 53, 55

H

hate crime, 6, 8, 25, 50
  by the numbers, 15
  causes and effects,
    25–38
  definition of, 6, 8
  examples of, 12, 14,
    18, 20, 22, 28, 30, 32,
    35–36, 38
  history of, 7, 16
  ideologies, 40, 44, 50,
    82, 94
  impact of, 32, 33–35
  legislation, 16–17
  responding to, 53,
    56–73

root of problem, 7
  types of, 10–14, 16
  underreported, 61
Hate Crime Help, 61
hate crimes statistics, 6
hate groups in the US,
    39–55
  categories of, 39
historic symbolism, 13
hollaback!, 55
homicide, 8, 14
hope for future, 91, 93

I

"Innovate Against Hate,"
    79
intolerance, 78

J

James Byrd Jr. and
    Matthew Shepard
    Hate Crimes
    Prevention Act (2009),
    22, 24
Jones, Arthur, 51–52

K

King Jr., Dr. Martin
    Luther, 84, 91
Ku Klux Klan (KKK), 18,
    39, 40, 42, 48, 87

L

LGBTQ people, hate crimes against, 13, 22, 42, 59
living in culture of hate, 52–55

M

mainstream politics, 44, 47, 52
Mandela, Nelson, 74
myths and facts, 23–24

N

National Center for PTSD, 33, 65
nationalism, 40
neo-Nazi, 39, 40, 42–43, 44, 50

O

Obama, Barack, 22, 93
online harassment, 8, 10, 12

P

Parks, Rosa, 38
post-traumatic stress disorder (PTSD), 6, 64–65, 70

symptoms of, 34–35
prejudice, 7, 8, 31, 53, 72, 78
Public Religion Research Institutes, 76

Q

questions to ask, 94–95

R

race, 6, 8, 10, 15, 16, 18, 31, 40, 42, 45, 62, 70, 76
racial bias, 28, 40
racial slur, 4, 95
racism, 14, 24, 36, 40, 72, 76, 83, 84, 87, 88
rape, 8, 13–14
religion, 8, 10, 15, 18, 62, 74, 90
religious bias hate crimes, 15, 31
resources, 7, 53, 56, 61, 63, 66, 68, 83

S

sexual assault, 8, 13–14
sexual orientation, 6, 8, 10, 15, 22, 31
Shepard, Matthew, 20, 22, 24

social courage, 72, 78
social media, 10, 12, 62, 73, 79, 82
Southern Poverty Law Center (SPLC), 39, 43
stereotype, 38
symbolic acts, 8, 12, 13
systemic oppression, 40, 68, 60

T

take action task list, 82–83
Till family, 35–36, 38
Trump, Donald, 44–45, 47, 50, 52, 55
Tubman, Harriet, 84

U

"Unite the Right" rally, 47–48, 50
Urban Mediamakers, 76

V

vandalism, 6, 8, 12–13
verbal abuse, 8, 10–11
Victim Connect, 61
victims of hate crimes, 56
acknowledge it, 56, 58
cope, 56, 58
coping with trauma and

PTSD, 64–65
reach out, 62–63
record it, 58

 W

white supremacy, 40, 47, 48, 51
who commits hate crimes, 25
crusaders, 28, 30
defenders, 26
retaliators, 28
thrill seekers, 25–26
women, 13–14, 84, 86
working with hate crime victims, 65–66

 Y

Yousafzai, Malala, 84, 86

About the Author

A Chicago native, Jill Robi is an entertainment journalist with a BA in the literary arts. A self-proclaimed geek, Robi is a movie aficionado and film critic, avid comic-con attendee, and cosplayer. As an African American woman, she feels passionately about the topic of hate crimes and believes there are some things that simply must be discussed.

Photo Credits

Cover, pp. 40–41 Anadolu Agency/Getty Images; pp. 4–5 ansem/Shutterstock.com; p. 9 Oleg Doroshin /Shutterstock.com; pp. 10–11, 46–47 Daniel Leal-Olivas /AFP/Getty Images; pp. 16–17, 92 Bettmann/Getty Images; p. 19 Steve Liss/The LIFE Images Collection/Getty Images; p. 21 Joseph Sohm/Shutterstock.com; pp. 26–27 David McNew/Getty Images; pp. 28–29 Leonard Zhukovsky /Shutterstock.com; p. 33 amenic181/Shutterstock.com; p. 37 Afro Newspaper/Gado/Archive Photos/Getty Images; p. 43 Ditty_about_summer/Shutterstock.com; pp. 48–49 Pool/Getty Images; pp. 54–55 Krakozawr/E+/Getty Images; p. 57 Anneka/Shutterstock.com; pp. 60–61 Photographee .eu/Shutterstock.com; pp. 63, 68–69 wavebreakmedia /Shutterstock.com; p. 71 Martin Godwin/Hulton Archive /Getty Images;p. 75 Per-Anders Pettersson/Hulton Archive/Getty Images; pp. 76–77 Monkey Business Images /Shutterstock.com; pp. 80–81 Michael Kovac/Getty Images; pp. 84–85 Richard Stonehouse/Getty Images; pp. 88–89 betto rodrigues/Shutterstock.com.

Design and Layout: Nicole Russo-Duca; Editor: Rachel Aimee; Photo Researcher: Ellina Litmanovich